Apes

CONTENTS

© Aladdin Books Ltd 1986

Designed and produced by
Aladdin Books Ltd
70 Old Compton Street
London W1

First published in the
United States in 1987 by
Gloucester Press
387 Park Avenue South
New York NY 10016

Printed in Belgium

ISBN 0-531-17038-1

Library of Congress Catalog
Card Number: 86-82691

Certain illustrations have previously appeared in the ''Closer Look''
series published by Gloucester Press.

The consultant on this book, JL Cloudsley-Thompson,
is Professor of Zoology, Birkbeck College,
University of London, UK.

Apes

MICHAEL FITZPATRICK

Illustrated by
RICHARD ORR

Consultant
J. L. CLOUDSLEY-THOMPSON

Gloucester Press
New York · Toronto · 1987

Apes, monkeys and Man

Apes, monkeys and ourselves are all members of the primate animal family. There are 193 different species or types of animal in this family group. The apes and monkeys are nearest to us in appearance, intelligence and in many of the things they do. They are our closest animal relatives.

Close links

In relation to their body size, apes have larger brains than any other creature except us. Some apes have shown great ability at learning and imitating human behavior, including language. By using signs like those used by deaf-and-dumb people, scientists have been able to teach several gorillas to express feelings and ideas. Koko, an ape who has been learning sign language for 12 years in the United States, can chat, tease, make jokes and even tell lies.

Mountain gorillas are members of the ape family whose survival is in danger. Their natural habitat is being destroyed by man.

Survival

Despite these close links with our primate cousins, apes are among the many species of animal whose survival is in danger because of the activities of humans. Their jungle homes are being destroyed for timber and to clear land for farming. Many are killed for sport by hunters. Consequently, their future is uncertain.

Primates

There have been primates on the Earth for the past 70 million years. Today they range from tiny, rat-like creatures such as the tree shrew, all the way to the most intelligent primates of all, human beings.

There are many differences between the types of animals in this group, but all primates share a number of common features. Primates tend to feed during the day and rest at night; they have a highly-developed sense of sight, with eyes that can judge distance; primate hands have fingers that are jointed and can be used for gripping; most have nails rather than claws; and most primates are "omnivorous," which means they can eat any kind of food, both meat and vegetation.

Primate groups

The least-developed primates are called "prosimians." These creatures, like the lemur and the tarsier, are night hunters who eat mainly insects. Next come the monkeys, which can be divided into two groups, "New World" and "Old World," depending on where they have developed.

Lemur

Tarsier

Tree shrew

The prosimians are the smallest primates. They share many characteristics with monkeys and apes, but are more closely related to more primitive animals.

Spider monkey

Capuchin monkey

The New World monkeys are found in Central and South America. They have wide nostrils and long tails.

Baboon

Colobus monkey

The Old World monkeys are found in Africa and Asia. They have narrow snouts and tough pads of skin on their rumps. These allow them to sit feeding for hours.

The advanced primates

The most advanced primates are divided into three groups: the gibbons, the Great Apes, and Man. The gibbons are small and spend all their time in the trees. The Great Apes – orangutans, gorillas and chimpanzees – divide their time between the trees and the ground and are all highly intelligent.

Gibbon

Chimpanzee

The gibbons and the Great Apes have no tails. All are expert climbers who spend at least part of their time in the trees. All can walk upright.

7

Primate development

By examining the very old remains of animals which are called "fossils," scientists have learned about the earliest primates and how they have developed.

Seventy million years of change

The oldest prosimian fossils so far discovered are the skeletons of insect-eating animals that lived in Europe and North America about 70 million years ago.

Fossils from 30 million years later show that some prosimians changed over time. The bones of the hands and feet became better for gripping. The eyes moved from the side of the head to the front, making distances easier to judge precisely. As the changes continued, the prosimian snout became shorter, sight became more important than smell, and the primates began to walk with their heads raised, looking about instead of sniffing the ground.

These skeletons of a macaque monkey, a gorilla and a human show how their structures have adapted to different ways of life. The macaque can walk along narrow branches; the gorilla can stand up to look for food; a human's straight back and strong legs are ideal for walking upright.

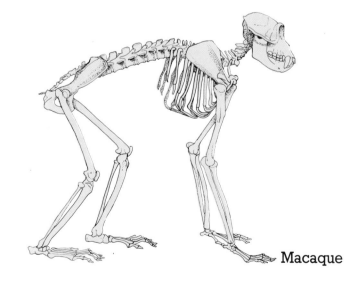

Macaque

Shape and purpose

As a result of changes over millions of years, the physical shape of monkeys, apes and humans is quite different today. Monkeys have long, narrow bodies with legs and arms of about the same length. They usually walk on all fours and some can use their tails for gripping, like a fifth hand. Apes use their long arms for balance, while humans have adapted totally to walking upright.

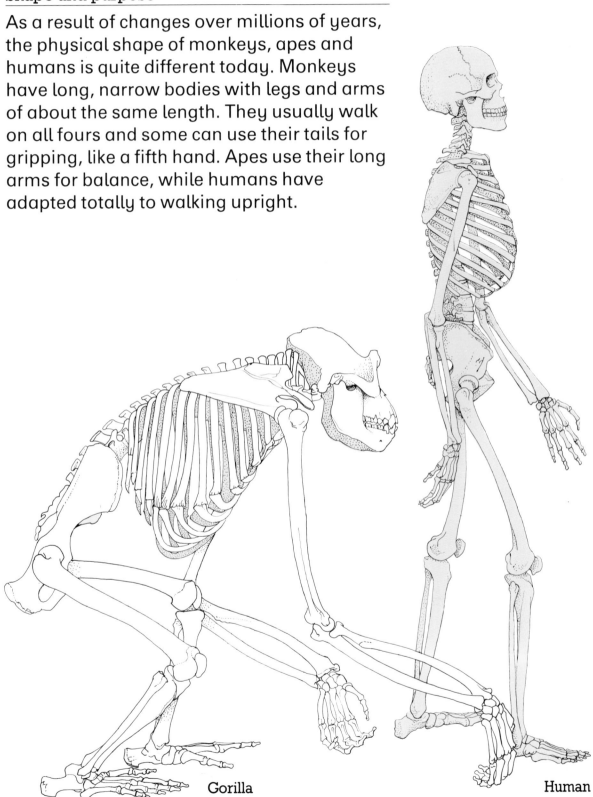

Gorilla

Human

9

Similarities and differences

The physical similarities between apes and humans are very striking. But it must be remembered that apes are "quadrupeds," or four-footed animals, that sometimes stand upright. Man is the only primate that always walks on two feet.

The brain

Human beings differ from the apes most clearly in the development of the brain. Our larger brains allow us to remember more, figure things out more quickly and to learn from our experience. No other animal has developed art and literature!

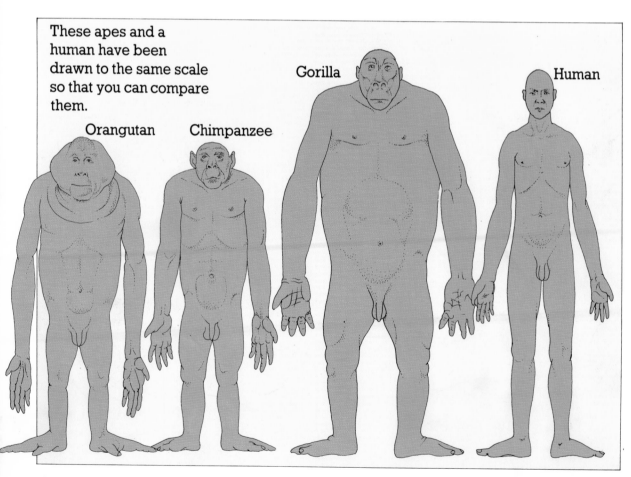

These apes and a human have been drawn to the same scale so that you can compare them.

Orangutan

Chimpanzee

Gorilla

Human

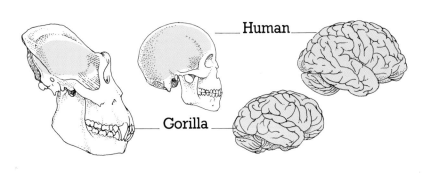

Human

Gorilla

The human brain, which measures 1,300 cubic centimeters (79.4 cu. in.), is much larger and a lot more powerful than that of even the largest ape.

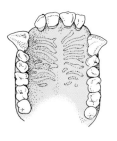 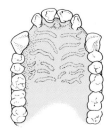 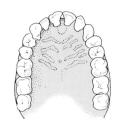

Chimpanzee Gorilla Human

Apes have exactly the same number of teeth as humans. Human teeth are arranged in an arc, while those of the apes form three sides of a rectangle.

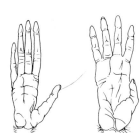   

Gibbon Orangutan Chimpanzee Gorilla Human

Apes and humans have "opposable" thumbs. This means that the thumb can be moved at an angle to the fingers, giving great strength to the grip.

Gibbon Orangutan Chimpanzee Gorilla Human

The feet of gibbons, orangutans and chimps all have opposable big toes for climbing. The gorillas are losing this feature.

Gibbons

Long fingers, light bodies and flexible shoulders allow gibbons to swing from arm to arm through the trees. This method of traveling is called "brachiation."

☐ Gibbon
☐ Siamang

The gibbons are the smallest of the apes. There are seven different types. The largest, the Siamang, is less than 1m (3 ft) tall. Adult males weigh about 6kg (13 lb). The gibbons make their homes in Southeast Asia, where they eat fruit, nuts, insects and small birds.

Noisy acrobats

Gibbons live in small family groups, defending their territory against other families by means of very loud cries of warning. The Siamang actually has a vocal "sac" like a balloon in its throat. This swells up and helps make the cry louder. It can be heard nearly a mile away.

With their long arms and light bodies, the gibbons are also excellent climbers.

The acrobatic gibbons can swing from branch to branch at great speed and they can easily jump across gaps of seven meters (23 ft). This means that they seldom risk meeting predators on the ground.

Gibbons have opposable toes. Using their long arms like a tightrope-walker's pole, they can run easily along narrow branches. They walk on two legs on the ground.

Gorillas

Despite their large and fearsome appearance, gorillas are the gentlest of the apes. They live in Central Africa, generally in groups of about fifteen, with one adult male as leader.

Both Lowland and Mountain gorillas have similar habits. The mountain type has a heavier, shaggy coat.

Peaceful vegetarians

Gorillas eat only fruit and plants. To get enough nourishment from this vegetarian diet, they spend most of their time and energy eating.

■ Mountain gorilla
☐ Lowland gorilla

The tiny area occupied by the Mountain gorillas is becoming steadily smaller every year.

The great silverback

Silverbacks

Gorillas can live to be 40 years old. Between the ages of ten and fourteen, the black hair on the back of the male slowly turns gray. After this he is known as a "silverback."

Leadership

The leading silverback in a group maintains order, usually by grunts and nudges. He decides where the group will rest and feed, and when and where they will sleep. If the group is in danger, the leader will try to frighten the intruder by roaring or performing his "display." If necessary, he will charge at the attacker, using his great strength and size.

This young gorilla has the small ears and broad nose with wide-set nostrils typical of its species. Both sexes mature between six and nine years. Males do not reach their full height until they are twelve.

The display is the male gorilla's way of showing annoyance. First he starts hooting. Then he puts a branch in his mouth, stands upright, and hurls leaves into the air. He drums on his chest, kicking with his legs, and then runs around, tearing at the vegetation.

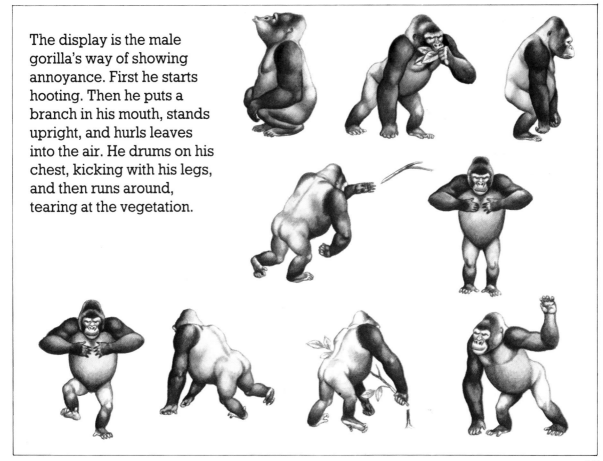

Life in the forest

Gorillas take life easy, eating and sleeping. Man is their only real enemy.

Gorillas are "nest-builders." The females climb high into the trees and make sleeping platforms by bending branches inward and covering them with leaves, moss and dirt. This provides a safe place for their young to rest. The heavier males sleep on the ground.

A safe future?

There is a real risk that these gentle creatures may soon be wiped out completely. Pressure from hunting and farming has forced the gorillas higher into the mountains, away from the plants they most like to eat and into a much smaller and poorer area.

The great amount of
vegetation which a
gorilla chews each day
is often very coarse and
damaging to its teeth.
Many older gorillas
suffer from tooth decay.
The first picture below
shows that many
chewing teeth have
fallen from this old
gorilla's mouth.
Chimpanzees have
some dental trouble too,
caused by fruit acid.

Gorilla

Chimpanzee

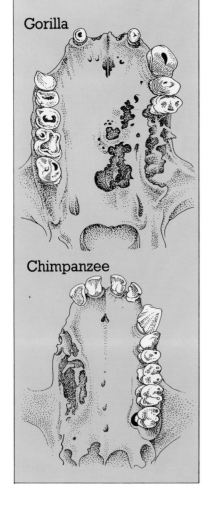

There may be fewer than
5,000 Mountain gorillas left
alive today. They have
thick, hairy coats which
keep out the cold in their
high homeland.

Orangutans

In Malay, the language of Malaysia, orang-utan means "the old man of the forest." Once widespread in the rain forests of Southeast Asia, the orangs too are facing extinction. There may be only 5,000 left.

Orangutan

Strange features

The mature male orangutan is quite distinctive. He has a large pouch under his chin, and fleshy "blinkers" at the sides of his face. The pouch is used for making loud warning noises.

Orangutans sometimes live in small family groups, but are also seen alone.

21

The slowest apes

Because they are not good tree swingers, orangs are called imperfect brachiators.

If an adult male orangutan stood up straight, he would be 1.25m (4ft) tall. Orangs' arms are much longer than their legs and have a total span of well over 2m (7ft).

Orangs eat mainly fruit. Like the gorillas, they are nest-builders, both males and females spending the night on platforms above the ground.

Careful climbers

Although orangutans can travel quickly when they have to, they usually move very slowly through the jungle. Careful climbers, they are the slowest of the apes which makes them easy to catch. Catching or owning an orangutan is illegal. Yet poachers hunt and sell young orangs as pets.

There are known to be many orphan baby orang-utans in the wild. Their mothers have been captured or killed by hunters. Only one out of every five infants captured will survive.

22

A puzzling creature

Scientists are trying to answer many questions about the orangutan. No one is sure how the young behave after they leave their mothers. They may form small groups before going off to live alone.

Male orangs are much larger than the females but no one is quite sure why. Since these are peaceful, solitary creatures without natural enemies, the extra size is unlikely to be for defense.

Orang "language" may be very advanced, but it is difficult to investigate since these are such rare and shy creatures. Scientists have rarely been able to hear the sound wild orangs make.

The male orangutan changes with age. First, he develops side flaps on his face, then the throat pouch.

Chimpanzees

The chimpanzees are the most intelligent of the apes. There are four different types. They are all similar in their habits and all, except the smaller pygmy chimpanzee, are similar in appearance. They live mainly in the jungles of West and Central Africa.

Daily life

These apes live a quiet, fruit-gathering life. They roam the forests in mixed groups with the adult males searching to locate food for the others. Chimpanzees eat nuts and berries and can survive on a very varied diet.

☐ Chimpanzee

Chimps do not defend a special territory and different groups mix quite freely.

Chimpanzee society

Mothers with infants are shy. They rely on the older males to find their food and tell them where it is. The size of most groups deters predators.

The more noise a male chimp makes, the more important he is. Sometimes males can be heard 5km (3 miles) away.

A chimpanzee group may contain up to eighty individuals. The whole group wanders over a very large area of jungle, especially when food is scarce.

Unlike the gorillas, chimpanzees do not travel as a community following one leader. But their groups do have dominant males. These chimps gain their status or importance by means of displays that look like temper tantrums. They scream, uproot small trees and throw rocks. The noisiest, most violent males are the most important in the group.

The friendly apes

Young chimps stay with their mothers for about six years. Daughters stay longer and seem to keep in touch with their mothers, even after they have children of their own.

Although chimpanzees do not use words, they can communicate with each other by means of grunts and facial expressions.

Excitement

Fear

Anger

Joy

Sadness

Because they build a new nest every night, breaking and bending the branches of their chosen tree, nesting chimpanzees can do a great deal of damage in the forest. Young chimps play at nest-building from a very early age.

Chimpanzee intelligence

Chimpanzees have a high level of curiosity and many abilities once thought to belong only to humans. They are able to use simple tools. For example, they poke sticks into termite mounds for food. They also use stones as weapons, throwing them at their enemies to drive them away. They soak leaves in water and then squeeze them like a sponge in order to drink.

Making a bed

Each chimp makes a new nest every night. The work normally takes only about five minutes. When the nest is ready, the chimp will try it out, often sitting up to put a handful of moss over a bumpy bit.

Chimpanzees use slender sticks to poke into a termite mound. When the insects grip the stick, they are pulled out and devoured.

Captive chimps

Chimpanzees in zoos have shown other sides of their natural intelligence. In one experiment, a banana was hung out of a chimp's reach. An adjoining room contained several boxes. The chimp collected and built up the boxes and climbed up to reach the fruit.

Artists and technologists

Some zoo chimpanzees have shown an interest in drawing and painting. They love examining complicated equipment like cameras, and are very good at solving practical problems. If food is locked in one box and the key to the food in another, captive chimps can learn how to reach the food.

Both chimpanzees and orangutans hurl weapons at intruders. Chimps are relatively free from attack by predators, but they often drive away competing baboons by throwing stones at them.

Savanna chimpanzees

In the savanna, chimpanzees have had to become hunters and meat-eaters in order to survive.

Not all chimpanzees live in the rain forest. Many live in the open woodland at the edges of the vast African grasslands known as the savanna. Here, the fruit trees are very far apart. There are many other animals also searching for food. Some of these, like the lion, the leopard and the python, hunt and kill chimpanzees to eat. Despite these dangers and difficulties, savanna chimps survive.

The hunting apes

One of the most surprising discoveries among savanna chimps is the fact that they kill other animals for food. Perhaps because fruit is so scarce, these chimps have been known to kill monkeys, baboons, young antelope and other small creatures so that they can eat the meat.

Adapting to new surroundings

Of all the Great Apes – gorillas, orangutans, chimpanzees – only the chimps move into new habitats or surroundings, and adjust to a different life and new types of food. Therefore it is not really surprising that the number of gorillas and orangutans continues to decline, while the world's chimp communities successfully thrive.

Our responsibility

The spread of the human race is the main reason for the current threat to the future of the apes. National parks have been set up to protect endangered animals. But such reserves cost a lot of money – unfortunately more than the African and Asian nations can afford.

To see over the tall grass, the savanna chimps stand upright.

Glossary

Brachiation   The method of traveling by swinging with the arms through the trees from branch to branch.

Fossils   The ancient remains of bones or tools that have been preserved in rock.

Great Apes   The gorillas, orangutans and chimpanzees are known as the Great Apes. The gibbons are simply apes.

Habitat   The natural surroundings in which an animal lives.

New World   North and South America.

Old World   Europe, Africa, Asia and Australasia.

Predator   An animal which hunts and kills others for food.

Primates   The large group of 193 animal species which includes prosimians, monkeys, apes and human beings.

Prosimians   The smallest and least-developed members of the primate group.

Quadruped   Any creature which walks on all fours; four-footed.

Savanna   The tropical grasslands of Africa.

Vegetarian   Any creature which eats only plants and their fruit; not meat-eating.

Index